An MTW Guide

RAISING
SIGNIFICANCE
A GUIDE TO RAISING INDEPENDENT,
WELL-ROUNDED AND CONFIDENT KIDS

MICHELLE TAYLOR WILLIS

An MTW Guide

RAISING
SIGNIFICANCE

A GUIDE TO RAISING INDEPENDENT, WELL-ROUNDED AND CONFIDENT KIDS

MICHELLE TAYLOR WILLIS

GAGNANT MEDIA

ATLANTA

An MTW Guide

RAISING SIGNIFICANCE

A Guide to Raising Independent,
Well-Rounded and Confident Kids

Written by
Michelle Taylor Willis

Presented by
Gagnant Media

The fonts are Avenir 10pt., 12pt., and Charter. Michelle offers words of
enlightenment for raising children with intention and ideas for whom we
believe and hope they can be.

Copyright 2020 © Michelle Taylor Willis
Cover Photo by Pitter Productions Photography
Inside Author Photo by Nick Nelson
Jacket Author Photo by Studio Whimsical Photography

ISBN 978-0-578-79407-5

Library of Congress
1. Parenting 2. Kids and Parents 3. Parenting Self-Help

Hard Cover

Printed in the United States

DEDICATION

This book is dedicated to my four boys—Trae, Braedon, Triston and Pace. You are better humans than I could ever be. Thank you for giving me great content to produce this book.

ACKNOWLEDGEMENT

I'd like to first thank God, who constantly reminds me that I am absolutely the person He created me to be. Of course, I must thank Sir Willis (I knighted him myself), for whom without his partnership this book could not have been possible, for more reasons than the obvious. Also, a huge shout out to my mother, who raised someone who was able to raise others, and to my sisters who always have a loving way of reminding me that I'm a much better parent than I am sister ☺. Thank you for always supporting me; I can only hope that I give more support than I get.

Thank you to my extended family who support me in everything I do. Also, I'd like to thank my closest circle of friends, who consistently challenge me to live out my purpose. A special thanks to Ms. Gloria. Thank for your patience and for hanging around after I kept having kids!

Thank you to my staff at Gagnant Media and MTW Enterprises, who provide me direction and energy to stay focused. This book may not have happened if they hadn't convinced me that the world needs this information.

Finally, thank you to my followers and supporters, old and new. I would not be where I am if you had not believed in me.

FORWARD

When Michelle approached me to read this book, I expected nothing less than a thoughtful and practical strategy to raising children. She assisted me with building my business, and mediocre is just not her way. Additionally, I have had the great opportunity of caring for her children, who are exceptional young people. So, it completely made sense for her to write a book on "raising significance," as everything I've ever known her to do had purpose and significance.

"How do I get my child to follow directions?" "She's making good grades, but what else will help her get into medical school?" "He just plays video games all day, and I'm not sure what to do." "I need help!" These are just a few of the questions and statements I've been asked or told over the past 9 years of my practice. As a board-certified pediatrician, I am expected to help guide families in raising healthy, kind, and productive children. Though there is more than one way to accomplish this goal, there are some basic rules, which consistently result in raising good, decent, and exceptional human beings.

This book provides a winning recipe for raising children. Remember, with any recipe, you can add and remove ingredients to best suit your taste; but there must be a starting point. This book provides a great starting point and recipe for growing and developing young minds.

I invite you to sit back, read, learn, and enjoy what may be one of the most crucial pieces of material you will read to raise your children to be significant!

— *Tiffini Billingsly, MD FAAP*
Pediatrician and Owner
Premier Pediatric Associates, PC

PROLOGUE

Raising Significance is an easy-to-read guide for parents wanting to instill basic principles in their children. Michelle has done an incredible job of providing step-by-step instructions for how parents should train their children at young ages and give them principles that will last a lifetime. I am a parent of two grown children and I know how important it is to be intentional about raising children and leaving a legacy for them and through them.

As a judge that has routinely been face-to-face with misdirected children and exhausted parents, I know firsthand what it looks like when children have no direction or are misguided. I remember one case when...

As I read Michelle's book, I'm reminded of that case and many others where parents just needed help, and kids needed the proper guidance and supervision, often someone to pour love into them. A resource like Michelle's book that isn't too overdone with fancy words and is made for the common reader would have been a perfect solution. If I had Michelle's book in those circumstances, I could have given it to those parents to help redirect their parenting efforts, and help instill confidence in them as parents communicating with their children.

In the times in which we are living now, we have more access to our children's lives than ever. Resources like *Raising Significance* can be used to empower our children and arm them with tools that can impact their lives forever, as well as, take them from being mediocre to truly significant.

Michelle uses humor, transparency and real life experiences to craft a book that is fun, informative and educational. I count it as a must read for any parent and anyone who plans on being a parent. Well done, Michelle!

— *Judge Penny Brown Reynolds*
Author, Public Speaker & Social Justice Advocate

FIRST WORD

THIS IS WHERE IT ALL BEGINS

"What kind of kids do you want to raise? Contributing members of society? Game changers?"

What kind of kids do you want to raise? Contributing members of society? Game changers? I'm hoping you said *game changers*. The former is good—don't get me wrong—but the latter, well. . .do I need to explain? This book will give you some key points to raising game changers. And, here's the kicker: It's not rocket science! These are tried and true methods. They've worked for me and lots of other parents—I've seen it firsthand. You may already be implementing some of these concepts, but when you put them all together, they have a synergistic effect of sorts. Trust me on this. *And why should I trust you, M.T. Dubbs?* you might ask.

Well. . .allow me to introduce myself. *"My name is H...!"* Okay, it's not, but I do love that song! I am Michelle Taylor Willis, a Florida native who migrated to Atlanta. I'm a wife and mother of four boys, and happen to run a couple of businesses in my spare time. People see my kids and often ask how I get them to do this or that, how they speak several languages, how they make their own meals, etc. Why are they so happy all the time and so well-behaved? The answer is easy: it's purely training and being intentional about what I teach and expose them to—periodt. (The "t" is supposed to be there)!

I remember when my oldest was young, and he would wake up super early on the weekends. I was trying to sleep in because, you know, I worked all week and was tired. This was when I was still in corporate America. On one Saturday, I was fed up with him waking up at 6am, so I showed him how to put frozen waffles in the toaster; he was maybe 4 or 5 (at the time). I was a divorced mother, and split our kid time with my ex-husband. My son caught on quickly. From there, I would pour orange juice in a cup at night, so his drink was ready for him the next morning then I'd prepare the TV. "Iron Giant" was the movie of choice back then which is a great movie! I'd put the movie in the DVD player, set the TV on the right input, and lay the remotes out. I taught him how to press *play* and turn the TV on, adjust the volume, and voila! From that point on, I just kept adding tasks, and before I knew it, he was making his own breakfast, cleaning bathrooms, cleaning the house, reading and learning all kinds of things sooner than most. I've continued adding different skills with each kid, and not only has it saved my husband and me a lot of time, but I've seen how these kids have become less dependent on me for just about everything. They have become so well-rounded in so many things. They are great students, athletes, musicians, chefs, friends, linguists, techies . . . they can do so much stuff! It's crazy! They are also sweet, charming and funny humans. I often say that my children are better humans than I will ever be, and I am pretty great, so that's saying a lot! (I'm really not, but it's still saying a lot)! :)

There are literally just a few things you need to know to do the same with your children. Are there more? Sure! But if you implement these basic rules, anything else will be a bonus. I guess I could come up with a Volume 2, but first things first. In this quick read, I'll show you a lot about what you need to know to raise well-rounded, confident, independent kiddos. And, oh yeah, they're pretty happy, too!

Let me just say, I'm not a doctor, mental health professional, accredited child expert, or any other certified professional. I'm just a mom who has happened to raise better humans than I could ever be (and I'm not the only one who thinks so.) I've had conferences where I've taught these concepts. Parents reach out afterwards and tell me, "I'm using Rule One. It's great!" My friends have been using my rules and asking me for advice for years. I am by no means a perfect parent, and my kids are not perfect kids. I'm sure I'm doing a fine job of screwing them up to a certain degree. I mean, isn't that what we as parents do? But some of this I have gotten right.

I'd like you to keep one thing in mind: A key to all of this is to **intentionally** teach them these skills **as early as possible.** If you have older kids and you're just getting this book, it's never too late, so start as soon as you possibly can. Okay, let's dance!

CHAPTER 1

OBEY IMMEDIATELY AND HAPPILY

"What's the first thing you do on the first day or weeks of a new job?"

I am sure you've heard the old adage, "Train a child in the way he should go and he will not depart." It is actually from the Bible, as you may know—not that you have to be a Bible lover to get it, just providing a point of reference. Anyhoo. . .everything really boils down to training. Think about it: What's the first thing you do on the first day or weeks of a new job? You guessed it! Training. This is because employers need to get you acclimated to the way of doing things the right way—their way—as soon as possible. Can you imagine the disasters that would happen if Microsoft techs came in and just started issuing lines of code the way they wanted to? This would result in the Microsoft executives coming in three months later to unteach and then reteach? Believe it or not, it happens more than it should and not because people don't receive training. It is because everyone is a know-it-all, and they want to do it their way, and there is not always accountability and follow-up in training, so things go awry. But friends, that is not the point. The point is that the training is done ASAP to instill the rules, guidelines and the go-do's early, not to mention the expectations. We have to treat our kids the same way, as little employees. And as soon as they get spit out, they have to be trained to obey. And obeying is not enough. They need to obey immediately and happily. People will respond to their current environment accordingly, and so will kids.

I got this concept from a school that Sir Willis (my hubby, if you didn't put two and two together) and I visited some time ago. It was a Christian elementary school, and I must say that they had a lot of good ideas for parenting basics. Obeying immediately and happily was one of them. At the time, I only had my two oldest, who were 13 and 5, at which point I was looking for a school for my 5 year old. The Head Mistress of the elementary school was a middle-aged woman that was one sweet piece of candy (although I felt like she could have pulled that ruler out at any second and started rapping on piano keys) and basically said that everything starts with children understanding authority, and they have to be trained to obey that authority. They need to understand that they have to listen to their parents the first time, and if they don't, it could end in disaster. She further explained that they (the school) train all the kids starting in kindergarten with the expectation that they obey the first time and without hesitation. Hence "obey immediately and happily." Wow!! Mind blowing! The more I thought about it, the more I realized she was right, and the idea became more and more real to me. Kids don't just need to obey, but they need to do it *immediately*. And, to keep the parent's stress level down, they need to do it *happily*. How many times have you wanted to pull your hair out when you have to tell your kids three times to do something? Or better yet, they do what you say, but they stomp, whine or give you pushback.

They must listen. On a rudimentary note, it just makes sense. *You, child, must listen to me, parent. I run this house, not you. I pay the bills. I make sure you eat. I make sure you go to school. I clothe you. I care for you. I nurse you. I truck you around town to birthday parties. I let you play with your friends. I encourage you. I go to your sporting events. I meet with your teachers. I protect you. I listen to you when I don't want to . . . blah, blah, blah.* Insert a host of other sentences that pertain to your individual situation. I think you see where I'm going with this.

On a more serious note, your child listening to you is the way you protect and educate them. As parents, we just have a few jobs: to teach them, protect them, make them leaders, and return them to God (insert your deity here, or none at all) in as good or better shape than when they arrived here (thank you, Auntie Tracey). You remember what your child looked like as a baby? What is one word that you would use to describe them? Does *perfect* sound about right? So, the only way we can accomplish all those tasks is for them to listen to us.

On a much deeper note, protection is our job. Here comes the immediate part. I can't tell you how many times this has happened: You come downstairs or in the common area. Everyone is watching TV or coding or doing whatever else they're doing besides the crap they should be doing. You say, "Clean your room."

They respond, "Okay, Mom." You go about your business for a few moments, and then come back to find out that no one has moved. You repeat, "Come on guys, clean up. I need you to sweep, wash the dishes, and straighten up."

They reply, "Yeah okay, Mom."

You come back fifteen minutes later and still nothing. Now, you've lost your mind and Hell Raiser Mom has officially entered the building. Does this sound familiar? AND, in my house the mantra is absolutely *obey immediately and happily*. So why haven't they moved? Arrrrgggghhhh!

I have been teaching my kids this forever. Is it perfect? No. Does it work more often than not? Yes. I cannot imagine how few hairs I'd have left if I hadn't been instilling this theme in them for the past eight years.

If we tell our kids to do something, and they don't do it now, it could literally be the difference between life or death. I use this example with my kids: We are at the store and see a strange man walking towards the car. I say, "Get in the car." They still mill around the vehicle slowly. I repeat in a firmer tone, "Get in the car!" These fools still don't move quickly enough. By now, said weirdo has approached the car and robbed us, taken the kids, and carjacked us. He could have done anything. I'm not making these scenarios up, either. They happen everyday, and we see them on the news. It's unfortunate. I tell my kids this is an extreme example, but if you don't listen to me with the little things, then why would I expect you to be able to execute listening on a higher level?

What about internet safety? When I say, "Only go on approved sites. Don't talk to anyone on the kiddie sites you visit." I've got every warning and block on as much as we can. We have alerts for everything, but kids these days are tech geniuses, and I need them to not circumvent the system for their own protection. This mantra could literally save their lives. Am I being dramatic? Maybe. But again, I'm okay with my kids being a little scared. Some fear is good. It just is. And it's the fear of terrible things happening and the fear of ME that may keep them on this Earth for as long as they should be here.

A couple other reasons why they should OIAH (Obey Immediately And Happily):

1. Your sanity. I mentioned those hairs you have on your head. If you want to keep them for a while and your vocal cords, you'll teach this early. Wouldn't it be great to say, "Clean your room" once, walk away, and spend the rest of your day whistling Dixie? You have a higher chance of that if you teach them this. I remember I asked my mom once when I was about 13, "Why are you always yelling?" She responded in an exasperated tone, "When I say it once and nicely, you don't do it!!"

2. It trains them to respond to authority when they are out of your house. Hey, no one likes being told what to do. But the reality is we have to obey and sometimes just submit to authority. Teachers, school bus drivers, bosses—it is what it is. Now, they have to know to whom to listen, and when, and know the difference when they're being told what to do is right or wrong (that in itself is training), but at the end of the day, there are times when they must obey

someone else other than us, and it's up to us to teach them how to do it.

The key to this is to start it as early as possible (did I mention this already?). Like as soon as you start talking to them, start saying this. Let them know your expectation is that they obey immediately and happily always. Will they? Hell no (they will eventually, because they'll have no choice)! But they will do it more often than if they didn't have this mantra. We've always gotten compliments on how well-behaved our kids are and how well they listen. We may be at dinner and they get rowdy. I snap my fingers once, and they're back on track. It's not foolproof, but it generally works. Ever wonder why it's recommended to start kids speaking languages early? Because the younger the mind, the easier it is to train. It hasn't been clouded with crap that prevents them from learning. Good and bad habits—the earlier they're taught, the better they stick.

How to Implement

If your kids are very young, like five and under, just start telling them—this is what's going to happen. Sit them down and explain to them in plain English what your expectations are and what will be the result of them not doing it. I'm not here to tell you how to discipline, but however you do it, be sure it's effective and you stick with it, or this won't work. You must execute on the back end. When they don't respond quickly, ask them, "How do we obey?" They should respond like the perfect angels they are, "immediately and happily." Insert smiley face.

For older kids, 6 and up, do the same thing. Sit them down and let them know this is the new mantra. Again, establish clear expectations, with consequences of them not OIAH. AGAIN, FOLLOW THROUGH IS KEY, especially with older kids. It won't work if you don't have clear consequences for them not obeying immediately and happily.

CHAPTER 2

TELL THEM WHO THEY ARE BEFORE THEY BECOME THAT PERSON

"Positive affirmations are a thing."

Positive affirmations are a thing. I was about 26 when I got that concept. I had pieces of paper all around my house, hanging from the doorways. My BFF would come over and say, "Get this crap outta my face!" He's about 6 feet 4 inches, so I could see how that could have been annoying for him. In any case, I've been implementing this for the past 20 years. Whatever I want to become, I just start telling myself that and watch it begin to happen. This is also true for your kids. Now be careful, as this power can be used for good or evil!

Why?

The brain is a muscle, and so is the flesh. They both can be trained, and they work in sync. When they work together, it's beautiful. When they work against each other, it's disastrous. Here's what I mean: Whatever you tell yourself to do, your body will follow suit. If you train your brain to believe you like running and you're a strong runner, you will like running, and your body will follow suit. Why wouldn't it? It doesn't have a mind of its own. YOUR body has YOUR mind. It's the same for your kids. Find out what their passions are and start telling them who they are. Make them say it. They will turn into those people. I have watched it happen. Sometimes it's quicker, and sometimes it could take years, but it does work. You want to train your children to become whatever they are purposed to be. We have to teach our children to think about the type of people they'd like to become, and then, train their minds to start developing them into those types of people. Their bodies will follow suit.

What I Did

I started giving my kids affirmations from the time they were babies. I would say things like, "I am a soldier of God." Or "One day, everyone's gonna know my name. I am the leader. I am the victor. I am a success. I own the business. I code video games. I build robots. I own an NFL franchise." These are a mixture of what I wanted them to believe and what they want to do. I even say some of these affirmations in my life now. Like "My son will have the woman who's perfect for them." Or "My son makes great decisions." These are just ideas, but you have to tailor your children's affirmations to what you and your kids' needs and dreams are.

What it Teaches

This teaches children to build good, routine habits. Every night, we say prayers as a family, the kids brush their teeth, use the bathroom, go to bed, and we say affirmations. They say them, I say them and they repeat them back. But nobody has ever shunned having solid habits, have they? Also, it teaches them the possibility of things happening, that anything is achievable and that their thoughts, wishes, hopes and dreams are real.

Other things it instills:
- Positive mental outlook
- Goals
- Confidence
- Discipline.

CHAPTER 3

GET THEM PIANO LESSONS

"My kids have great memories."

When I was pregnant with these crumb snatchers, I played classical music. I learned early and studied the link between kids who did well in math, science, and music. I played classical music from the time they were born until they were about 2 or 3 every night at bedtime. After that, it was kind of touch and go, mainly because I didn't want it to be a crutch for them falling asleep, but I could have gone longer.

Why it Works

Think about it. On a very fundamental level, they have to learn how to add. All those notes have corresponding numbers. They have to add this many beats to that many beats, and then, hold for a certain amount of time, blah, blah, blah. Also, think about the recall and what it does for memory. Those synapses (nerve fibers) have to be going crazy. When you teach that kind of recall at a young age, it trains the brain to think critically very early. My kids have great memories. Photographic sometimes. It actually kind of sucks. They're like, "Remember when you said…" and then they repeat the day, the time, what I said, the impetus for it. Then they hit me with, "Remember?" *No, Son, I don't. I never took piano. My memory sucks.*

Piano is shown to be effective as the best instrument to learn first. If you learn that first, it makes all of the other ones much easier. I can attest to that. My 11 year old learned it, and he went on to teach himself the guitar. Another one (13) learned the piano, and he plays the sax and clarinet, as well. They all play the recorder, along with every other elementary school student known to man. Lol!

What I Did

I started my oldest son at five on the piano. Although he just plays recreationally now, he can still read sheet music and is quite the thinker. I have since started each of my kids at 4 or 5 years old. At that age, it is a ten-minute lesson. They work their way up to thirty minutes once a week and practice on their own for ten minutes a day under your direction and supervision.

What it Teaches

In addition to what I've mentioned already, it also teaches discipline. Having to practice every week under the gaze of an authority figure at an early age is huge. And then, they have to be disciplined enough to practice every day, with you at first. And then without you as they get older. I remember when my second son would just go practice on his own when he got home from school. My husband and I would beam when we would hear him. When we added the others to the mix, it was funny because we would often say, "Who's on the piano?" It was so cool because we never knew which of the three (the youngest was still really small) would be playing. We would sometimes be surprised to discover who was sitting in front of those keys.

I can remember one of my proudest moments was when my husband, my oldest (he was about 13 at the time) and I were in the mall. There was a baby grand in the middle of the walkway, unattended. I don't recall how he ended up there, but he just started playing Beethoven. I toyed with the idea of making him stop, but he attracted a small crowd and the actual pianist came back and just let him finish. He was so impressed by him and encouraged him to never stop. It was really cool! It would be a lot cooler if he still played, which he doesn't. But hey, you can't win them all!

Here are a few other cool things it teaches:

- Recall
- Addition
- Multiplication
- Rhythm.

What to Do

Ask around for referrals for a good piano teacher. I've got a resource page if you need one. Check at the school or with other parents. You can also check at local piano stores.

Don't buy a real piano unless you're sure it's gonna stick (which it should because they obey immediately and happily). To start, just buy a keyboard. It's a helluva lot cheaper and allows for space restrictions. Conversely, if your wallet and home will allow it, it never hurts to have a beautiful piano in your home. Pianos are great investments. I found my piano at a piano store on clearance fifteen years ago. It has lasted me four kids, and it's still going. The toughest thing about it is keeping it jelly and peanut butter-free.

CHAPTER 4

TEACH THEM A FOREIGN LANGUAGE

"Can you imagine your kids being able to go somewhere and know things most people don't know?"

Okay. The reasons why this is a good idea are endless. I'm sure you know a lot of them. However, knowing a language other than your native tongue makes ANYONE well-rounded. And it does wonders for kids.

Why?

Again, brain patterns. It teaches kids how to fire different synapses. Bottom line, whenever that happens, it can make you smarter. For young kids, it is a beautiful thing. It also instills confidence. Can you imagine your kids being able to go somewhere and know things most people don't know? I remember how my 11 year old son would feel so confident when he would speak Mandarin in public. I could literally see his tiny chest poke out. It was really important for him, because he had somewhat of the middle child syndrome, so he was always looking for ways to stand out. When kids can stand out among their peers, it gives them a little more confidence to stand up for themselves and others.

What it Teaches

Again, it teaches discipline. As I said before, it instills confidence, and makes them better thinkers. Critical thinking is a thing. It gives them a heads up among the other kids, and if they continue to develop it as adults, it makes them much more attractive in the job market, opening them up to larger opportunities.

What to Do

Immersion therapy here is always the best. Shoot, you may learn it too! There are several apps that can help with this, but always check with the school. Hopefully, they are getting exposed to foreign languages in school. If so, insist that the teacher speaks that language with your child in school, even if she doesn't with the other children. If you speak the language, then only speak that language with them, or speak it at certain times during the day.

What I Did

I speak French, so I just started speaking it with them as babies. I got books in French and read to them. In school, I always chose French as a language for them, along with any others that were available. We did Mandarin and Spanish also, but French was always a given. I usually speak it throughout the day, but around dinner time was the time of choice. At dinner, I usually speak in French and would mandate (for the most part) that they "Parlez et répondez en Français" (speak and respond in French).

Which Language?

If you have a native tongue, teach them that. I cannot tell you how many parents I meet that kick themselves for not speaking a language they know to their kids. Many of you are reading this right now thinking, *'That's me.'* If it is, start speaking in that tongue today. Remember, immersion is the best teacher. They have whole schools built on the immersion methodology.

It is also great to teach a language that you may not know, that way, you can be learning at the same time, which incorporates Rule #3. However, if you don't speak another language, you'll need to help them. They'll learn to practice every day and begin speaking the language at home, with your help. Check with the schools and see what language(s) they're teaching. Install apps to help them learn at home. Train them to practice ten minutes per day with or without your supervision. I like French. It's a point of differentiation. Most people don't speak it, so they'll stand out more and be seen as more exposed and well-rounded. And people will think you're the bomb-ass parent for being such a forward thinker! You're welcome. And French is expected to be the number one language in the world by 2050. How's that for thinking ahead? Any language will do. Make it easy on yourself. Choose something that will be easy for you.

CHAPTER 5

BRING THEM INTO YOUR WORLD

"Do we want the world to break the news to them, or should we?"

Let's be real. We spend a lot of time wrapping our lives around our kids. What do they want to eat? What activities are they involved in? What do they want to do this weekend? What chores do they want to do? What do they think? All of this makes sense and, to an extent, we need to do this. However, we need to be the first to let our children know that the world does not revolve around them. Do we want the world to break the news to them, or should we? Trust me, it's much less traumatic if we do it. Kids need to see how we operate rather than us always seeing how they operate. I remember a friend of mine telling me that he didn't feel engaged with his kids. He said they'd play video games and he'd always play sports and go to those events, but he wasn't getting any work done, and he felt like they didn't know what he did or what the real world was like.

That's when I told him this rule. I told him that during the time when he was going play games with them to instead bring them to his office and show them how he checks his email. Or have them listen to him make a phone call and take notes on the calls so he could use the notes for future communication with his clients. This would engage them because now he would be teaching them his world, which is helping him get his work done and also teaching them life skills. Both sides are fed. His kids would learn that it's not all about them, pick up skills about entrepreneurship, and literally spend quality time with their father. He wouldn't stop doing their stuff, they would just start doing his. Everyone wins.

Why?

They need to see how the world works. You are the world, for now at least. They need to understand that other things happen outside of them. This means us not giving in to their every whim and them figuring out things on their own. This means us telling them *no*. Now, they've been hearing *no* since they started crawling, for sure. But they can hear it more and learn different ways of getting the answers they want without always asking you.

If you're a working parent, and especially if you work for yourself, this is a great way to get your kids involved in what you do, and YOU WILL GET MORE WORK DONE. You can train them to do work. Maybe they could put stamps on envelopes, and if they're old enough, they can check your email. I've had my kids proof magazines. It teaches reading and comprehension. See where I'm going here? Win-win! Again, we get discipline training, and they get exposure. Remember—well-rounded, right?

How?

Think about the age level and figure out what they can do. Find age-appropriate tasks for them that will help you as well. I heard a financial advisor say that at a certain age you can actually put your kids on payroll. Check with your tax professional on that one, but what a great idea!

If you like certain activities, find ways to get your kids involved in those activities so that you can still do what you like. It helps you, and it's great for your kids as well.

What I Did

I tell the story often of how I put my kids on the swim team so they could learn how to swim laps. That way, they could go swimming with me at the gym, but they learn a life skill and become better athletes. And we got to hang out together! I have my kids work in the business. I mentioned earlier about them proofreading magazines. I have the little one shred papers or staple things together. I put the other ones on spreadsheets and office work. I give them tasks based on their age and skill level. My 21 year old now shoots videos and takes pics for me, while my 11 year old edits video. Oh yeah, I pay them also! They learn to value hard work and a little about earning their keep. Win-win-win! Is this making sense?

What it Teaches

You're teaching them long term to be out-of-the-box thinkers. You're also teaching them to be self-sufficient. They have to figure things out. Most importantly, they'll learn the sun doesn't rise and set on them. And, although we love them more than anything and they are the most important people to us, they learn and understand that we, the faithful parents, have to be taken care of as well and that self-care is important. They won't see that completely as children, but eventually they will.

Here's a few other things they learn:
- Entrepreneurship
- Work ethic
- Skills
- Self-discovery
- Organization.

CHAPTER 6

RAISE THEM TO BE INDEPENDENT

"How many people today can't cook, can't wash, can't even fulfill basic needs?"

Teach them early how to take care of themselves. For me, making waffles, washing and folding clothes, and developing life skills were big. When we hired a sitter to help out while I was in a corporate environment, I told her the things that I wanted to make sure my kids were learning and I hoped it matched with what she was teaching. I remember her sitting with my tiny kids, as she was teaching them how to fold clothes—sharing life skills. How many people can't cook, can't wash, can't even fulfill basic needs? Not on my (or my sitter's) watch! They need to learn how to do this stuff now, so they'll do it later! Fast forward, all my boys—even my 8 year old—wash and fold their own clothes. Sir Willis had the great idea to buy pods for the youngest, so he could put the detergent in. This was because one day we walked into the laundry room and there were suds everywhere. It looked like a picture from a Dr. Seuss book. Anyhoo, they all are domesticated boys and when they cook, their food is actually pretty legit.

Why?

The more independent they are now, the more likely they'll leave you when it's time. You won't be stuck with these kids forever, until they get their act together. I tell all the kids, *I've got you through college. After that, you're off my payroll and out of my house. Your rooms will be converted to studies or something.* I'm hoping this works! At the time of this writing, I've got about another year left of college for the oldest, so we'll see...

While they are in your house, you need to be able to do your own thing. How do you do that when you have kids pulling on you 24/7? It's not a thing. We, as adults and parents, have to be able to work, focus on home projects, or chill by ourselves uninterrupted! The only way to do this is to train your children to be able to do things on their own.

What I Did

I bring them in the kitchen to cook with me. I have them measuring and pouring, even at 3 and 4 years old. I give simple tasks, as young as age 2. I taught them to make beds early. You already heard the story about making breakfast. Make tasks easy for them. If they're too young to do something, break it down into doable chunks for them (reference my waffle story in the intro).

I taught my kids tasks early. Two things my mom told me to teach my kids right off the bat: reading and potty training. I taught them how to read early, so they could read independently of me. There's a book titled, *Teach Your Child to Read*. It was published in the 60's, but it is still very relevant. I used it with all of my children, per my mom's instruction, and they all read sight words by 2. So, when you tell them to go read at age 2, they go do it: Rules 1 and 6.

I also potty trained them from about 6 months old. I know it sounds crazy, but I used to sit these little tiny babies on the big toilet. I found this cool manual on how to potty train and used that (I actually expanded this method and created a book about it, which you can also buy). All of my boys were potty trained (daytime) by 18 months. This is no exaggeration: I've referred several of my friends and followers to this method. It's a pain in the ass for three days, but it works!

What They Learn

Quite simply, they learn everything. They learn as much as you teach them. But fundamentally, they'll learn how to do things on their own, without being told. They learn how to think. They also learn how to help you and others, which I love. You can assign them simple tasks that you may not want or have time to do. For example, I can say, "Triston, find out how I can revive my Easter Lily." And he'll bring the info back to me. Then, I can decide whether or not he's in a position to do the final task. They also learn, in my 11 year old's words, "You can't rely on everyone always; sometimes you've got to fend for yourself."

A few other things they learn:
- Discipline (this just keeps popping up, doesn't it?)
- Confidence
- How to take risks
- A host of life skills, depending on what you train them to do. For instance, cooking (math), reading, critical thinking, typing, emailing, communication skills, the list goes on and on . . .
- Creativity.

CHAPTER 7

FUEL THEIR PASSIONS

*"Do we need to give them another excuse to hate us if
we push them to do what we want?"*

I believe everyone has something they were born to do, a purpose. Your kids aren't excluded from that. An older parenting mentor of mine told me a while ago that whatever your children tell you they want to do, let them do it. (She also said don't ever buy what you think your kids want, just give them exactly what they ask for. That is one of the smartest things I've ever heard.) Of course, encourage education or whatever that looks like, but feed their passions and natural talents. We've all heard the story of how significant people who always wanted to be doctors, for instance, remember getting their first doctor's bag or Operation® game.

We all have ideas about what we want our kids to do, but if you push them to do what you want, even though they may be successful, they may not be significant. Worse than that, they'll be miserable and then blame you for it. Do we need to give them another excuse to hate us? I don't think so.

Why?

We want happy kids. Happy kids end up being happy adults, theoretically, of course. If your children are following their purposes and passions, the ones that they have established, then they are more likely to be compliant around those actions. For example, when you say, "Go read that anatomy book I just bought you," they'll be more apt to do so if they have a love of the human body. When you say, "I'm putting you in camp for three weeks this summer," they'll be excited to go if it's a robotics camp, and they love that stuff. This makes them happy.

This can also set them on a trajectory of what they may end up doing later. What great training! I share a story in the next section that illustrates this point.

What They Learn

They learn to trust their instincts and go with what they know. Do our guts fail us sometimes? Absolutely! But more often than not, it leads us down the right road. It also helps them figure out what they're good at and what they like. You can start developing what they think they like, and you may find out it's a *no bueno*, or you may find out it's a home run. Either way, you'll have a pretty good indicator.

Here's a couple of other things they get out of this:
- The knowledge that failure is sometimes eminent
- Commitment
- Discipline (there's that word again!)
- Confidence (are you surprised?)
- Creativity.

What I Did

I found out what they like. You probably won't have to ask. It should be evident, however, there are exceptions to every rule. If he's drawing everywhere, get him crayons or drawing kits. If she's always talking about the sun and the stars or space, get her books about that. You can encourage different things. For instance, I made all my younger three kids learn Scratch to code video games. One of them has veered away from it—no problem. He knows how, and I'm fueling other things in him. The other two are on it. One of them is a techie. He's taught himself JavaScript and other languages. He wins the tech fair every year, programs robots, blogs, writes and draws for comic books. So, we buy things in those spaces for him, look for camps that hone these skills, etc.

For instance, I started all my kids in acting as early as babies. I did it because I wanted them to be strong communicators and comfortable in front of the camera or people they don't know. I also wanted to build nest eggs for them to be able to invest in real estate or other businesses as adults. My 21 year old, who was in his first play around age 5 or 6, is currently still acting on and off, but at around age 10, he realized he liked operating the camera.

We gave him old video cameras and let him start shooting. I had him meet creators and camera operators, so that he could consistently learn. He created his first "Indy" film at 14. He filmed it at our house over a few days, and we literally had to create "sets" for him to use. The two younger boys were the stars. And age 16, he started his own video production company and now he's a Film Production major in college. He has produced video content for different companies—some pretty big—in Florida and Georgia.

As they get better in certain areas, it will raise a level of confidence in them, and it will make them happy!

CHAPTER 8

INVOLVE THEM IN TEAM SPORTS

"You want them to be independent and be able to work as part of a team."

Okay friends. The trick here is one at a time. You can't be driving all over town every day for two or three sports at a time. Well, maybe *you* can, but I won't! No way, José! If you want to expose them, do so, but just do it one sport a season until you figure out where they may land. *That's all I've got to say about that* (in my Forrest Gump voice).

I'm not saying there is anything wrong with solo sports, but there's a magic that happens when you have to learn to depend on team collaborations and working together. It's the individual's hard work for the benefit of the individual *and* the team, not one or the other.

Okay, let me break here for a second. Now, you may be saying, "But Michelle, you just told us you want them to be independent, and that you should raise independent kids! Now you want them to learn to depend on other people?!" Yes, smarty pants, I did. But that's because they need to be able to do things on their own without oversight, not because they're never going to have to work on a team. Now back to our regularly scheduled programming. . .

Nobody wants to hire someone who is myopic and can't play with the other kids in the sandbox. Team sports should be taught at an early age. Don't get me wrong, we *are* building independent children, and as I said before, they need to learn how to depend on themselves to a certain degree (see above rant). This is where some of the well-roundedness comes in, because team sports most certainly teaches them how to win. Vince Lombardi is credited for saying, "Winning isn't everything; it's the only thing." I agree and disagree. Winning is a thing, for sure. Everybody does not get a trophy, a medal, or a plaque. Friends, only winners get those. However, there is value in learning how to lose gracefully. Everybody takes an "L" sometimes—some more than others. Ahhhh, to the losers. But we don't want our kids to be that. So, let's focus on the #winning.

Why?

It keeps them busy. I'm not saying they won't get into any trouble, but the likelihood for it goes waaaaaay down. Kevin Hart's mom made him join the swim team to keep him out of trouble. A wise older woman once told me, "Baby, you better keep those boys busy. That will keep them outta these streets!" She's right. When my kids are in extracurricular activities, there's just not a lot of time to be chilling on the computer, game systems, or for any foolishness. Every minute of the day is scheduled. Actually, I can think of some adults whose every minute should be scheduled, too. Maybe their trouble meter would go down. But alas, that's a different story for a different day. You see what I mean, though?

There are LOTS of different personalities in teams, especially when you put kids together from different schools, neighborhoods, etc. What a great way to teach kids early how to deal with people different from them and then, to navigate through the differences. Some kids have brat parents, and some don't. Better to learn how to deal with assholes early in life. Kinda like losing! We try our hardest to shelter kids from hurt and pain, but we can't avoid it all. Some of it they need to get and get quick, especially if you are raising game changers.

What it Teaches

They learn negotiation skills—early. I know seasoned salespeople who couldn't negotiate themselves out of a bank robbery where the criminals had no guns and a cumulative IQ of 10. Critical thinking is at play here, too. When you have young minds working together to see how to be the best they can be, it's beautiful. It also teaches discipline and routine. Think about it. They have to go to school, come home, grab a snack, do homework, get ready for practice, go to practice, come home, eat dinner, go to bed, or in whatever order. They learn how to schedule at a young age, and discipline is wrapped in all of that. It carries over into later life, even if they veer away from it for a minute.

TIP: I'm circling back to this. PICK ONE SPORT A SEASON. It prevents burnout for you and them, and it gives them different things to do each season until they figure out what they like best. You can narrow it down to one or two a year until then.

Here are some other benefits they may gain from participating in team sports:
- Working with other people and personalities
- Experiencing the value of staying active and in shape
- Learning how to practice
- Scheduling
- Collaborating.

CHAPTER 9

SIBLINGS

"Every child is different!"

If you have one kid, you're set. But if you have two or more, let me say again, nothing is foolproof. One of the reasons for that is every child is different. I have four boys and over the years I have been reminded just how different they are from the clothes they like to the food they eat. And when it comes to the rules in this book, everything does not work for every parent, and everything will not work for every child. You need to understand that. So, don't come back to me saying, "Michelle, your book sucks. One kid is listening to me and the other is not. Thank you and good night." I'm forewarning you that you may need to tweak the rules a little for each kid.

One kid may jump on heavy to the affirmations, and one may take to the piano and still the other one may do better in foreign language. Understand the point here: we are teaching discipline, consistency, independence, and other life skills. We're not creating the next Mozart, (well maybe, if they're really good then we certainly are), or the next Mandarin professor. We are just breeding life-long skills in our children that will increase the likelihood that they will play a significant role in society. We are giving them a blueprint so that they will have opportunities to create better lives for themselves.

It's that simple and that complicated. Don't get bogged down in the details, friends. Remember why we are here. It doesn't matter that little Johnny doesn't sound as good as his brother, who sounds like he's from France when he speaks, or that he pronounces the language incorrectly. What matters is that he's being trained to use his brain differently. It may not matter that Janie (don't you love my original names for your children) doesn't become the astrophysicist that she said she may become in her affirmations, and that her sister does. What's important is that she believes, no, she KNOWS that her words matter, and that she believes she COULD do it if she wanted to. We are breeding SIGNIFICANCE, and these tenets are just ways to do it.

Now, to tie a little bow on this knot.

Here is how you can bring multiple children into this fold:

1. Everyone does the same thing. They all say affirmations. They all speak languages. They all take piano. They will all end up doing different things, and that is ok. Someone may end up on piano, someone may end up on sax, someone may end up on nothing (remember, because each child is different). But they're all being taught the same way. This is one way to keep order in your house and prevent yourself from going insane. And, as they get older, each child will teach the other one. Listen, there are so many times when I'll tell the 13 year old, "Go sit with your brother while he practices piano. Help him with his chords." I'm pretty sure I still don't know what a chord is, but what matters is that now I've got two kids out of my hair, (who knows where the other two are) while one is learning patience and how to teach, and the other is learning how to learn from anyone, and likely picking up how to play chords accurately. Win, win, and win. One of the things in life that we eventually learn is that teachers don't always look like teachers, and we can learn from anyone, anytime and anywhere. We just need to be open-minded.

2. Do as much together as possible. Say affirmations together, go to lessons at the same time, have them all working in your business, and even have them do chores

together. They may not be doing the same things, but they are likely together, in the same spaces. This is how they learn to work together and build a family. These kids can be fussing at each other one minute and preventing each other from killing themselves the next. This is a way they learn how to collaborate, and once again, they teach each other. I love it when my 8 year old is trying to sweep in one room, and the 11 year old comes in collecting trash. He sees the 8 year old holding the broom the wrong way, and says, "Turn it like this; it's easier." How awesome is that?! The blind leading the blind. I love it. But seriously, you see what's happening? They're all learning and teaching each other. The methods may be different, but the concepts are being instilled. And you, proud parent, are watching from afar with that smug smile on your face. Once again, you're welcome.

The only caveat here is that no one can deviate from Rule #1: OIAH. This is one rule that everyone gets, no questions asked. I don't care how different Ron is from Marie, who learns faster or slower, whatever. One thing everybody is going to get is how to follow Rule #1. No ifs, ands, or buts. My house, my rule. This is a mainstay through everything because without this, none of the other rules will work. Capiche?

CHAPTER 10

WINNING BEHAVIOR

"Is this foolproof?"

Well, that's all folks! It's not actually—it's just scratching the surface, but it is more than enough to get you and your kids on track to help them land where they need to be. Is it foolproof? Is anything? Again, some of this is built on science and some is not, but if you work on these concepts piece by piece, you will see changes in your life—and your children's lives.

You probably noticed that most of the skills that these rules instill are the same: confidence, discipline, well-roundedness. It's not by design. So much of who we are and what we become stems from these things. That's why we have to be intentional about training our children to have these qualities.

I have to admit, I was never the one to dream of being married and having kids. I had no idea what kind of parent I was going to be. I just knew I was going to be nothing like my mother: I wasn't going to yell at my kids, I'd never force them to make their beds, I'd let them stay in their pajamas all day, I'd let them eat as much sugar as they wanted, I'd NEVER make them drink fresh carrot juice, and I wouldn't be strict at all. Well, we know how that turned out! I'm just like my mother—maybe worse! But, she instilled things in me that were instilled in her, and I've instilled these things in my kids, even added on a little. And I'm hoping that you'll instill some of these ideas in your kids, too. So, get to it! Remember the first rule! Talk soon!

APPENDIX

RESOURCES

These resources are presented as additional information that may be helpful. The writer and publishers do not state that they endorse or share any specific ideas or beliefs as the information presented.

1. THE ADVENTURES IN PARENTING. https://www.nichd.nih.gov/publications/product/74. *Eunice Kennedy Shriver National Institute of Child Health and Human Development*, NIH, DHHS. (2001). Adventures in Parenting (00-4842). Washington, DC: U.S. Government Printing Office. Published 2001.

2. SEVEN TIPS FOR RAISING RESPONSIBLE CHILDREN: https://extension.usu.edu/news_sections/home_family_and_food/seven-tips-for-raising-responsible-children, University of Utah.

3. CORNELL COOPERATIVE EXTENSION: http://ccejefferson.org/parenting, Cornell University, Jefferson County, New York.

4. HOW TO HELP YOUR CHILD REALIZE THEIR BIG DREAMS. https://www.parents.com/parenting/better-parenting/how-to-help-your-child-realize-their-big-dreams/, Emma Sutton-Williams, November 15, 2019.

5. AMERICA'S CHILDREN IN BRIEF. KEY NATIONAL INDICATORS OF WELLBEING 2018. This scientific report offers federal statistical data on different aspects of children's health, such as poverty and exposure to violence. Report sponsored by NICHD. See a digital version of the report at https://www.childstats.gov/americaschildren/index.asp.

6. AN ACTIVITY BOOK FOR AFRICAN AMERICAN FAMILIES: HELPING CHILDREN COPE WITH CRISIS. https://www.nichd.nih.gov/publications/list/collection?g=7&col=13&cat=all. *Eunice Kennedy Shriver National Institute of Child Health and Human Development*, NIH, DHHS. (2012). An Activity Book for African American Families: Helping Children Cope with Crisis (03-5362B). Washington, DC: U.S. Government Printing Office. Published 2012.

7. Effectivechildtherapy.org. Developed through a partnership between APA Div. 53 (Society of Clinical Child and Adolescent Psychology) and the Association for Behavioral and Cognitive Therapies, this website offers information on the symptoms of and treatments for behavioral and mental health problems in children and adolescents. The site also helps parents determine whether a child's behavior is normal or is a sign of a bigger issue, and offers guidance on selecting a child psychologist.EVERYDAY PARENTING: THE ABCS OF CHILD REARING. https://www.coursera.org/learn/everyday-parenting. This free online parenting course was developed by former APA President Alan E. Kazdin, PhD, director of the Yale Parenting Center and Sterling Professor of Psychology and Child Psychiatry. The course provides 20 how-to videos explaining parenting techniques that address problem behaviors at home and school. In each video, Kazdin instructs parents on the importance of speaking to their children

in a calm or playful tone and allowing kids to make choices whenever possible. Kazdin also emphasizes the use of strategic and special praise.

8. HOW TO TEACH YOUR BABY TO READ. The Gentle Revolution Series. Written by Glenn Doman and Janet Doman. Six part book series highlighting subjects including math and intelligence. Available on Amazon via link @ https://www.amazon.com/dp/0757001858/ref=cm_sw_r_sms_api_i_vGwxFbZQF95DY.

9. SCHOOLHOUSE ROCKS! Aired January 6, 1973. Saturday mornings were filled with the songs that taught us everything from the Preamble to Adverbs, Verbs and Multiplication. These songs inspired our learning and helped us to remember with great songs like, "I'm Just A Bill." The 30th Anniversary version of the DVDs is available from Disney on Amazon.

10. AN MTW GUIDE: HOW TO POTTY TRAIN YOUR CHILD. Written by Michelle Taylor Willis. Copyright © 2020. Available on Amazon.

ABOUT THE AUTHOR

Michelle Taylor Willis, a Florida native now living in Atlanta, is married with four sons. She is an award-winning speaker, media personality, author, and entrepreneur, and is known around Atlanta as a master strategist and connector.

Michelle is the founder and owner of Gagnant Media and MTW Enterprises. She founded South Fulton Lifestyle Magazine, and is the host of the According to Michelle radio and tv shows. She chairs the Advisory Board for the United Way of Greater Atlanta (South Fulton), and serves as Chairperson for Theatre du Reve, the only french-

[Continued next page]

speaking theatre in America. She also serves on the Board of Directors for the South Fulton Chamber of Commerce, where she serves as the VP of Film and Entertainment. She was recently appointed to the Morris Brown College Foundation, and serves as Secretary. She also sits on the Board of Directors for both the Atlanta Aerotropolis Alliance and Atlanta CASA.

Michelle was named *"Outstanding Businessperson of the Year 2017" and "Small Business of the Year 2016"* by the South Fulton Chamber. She has been recognized as one of the "Top 100 Influential Women in Georgia and Atlanta" several times by different organizations, as well as one of the "Top 25 Most Powerful Women in Atlanta." Atlanta Business Journal recently named her as one of the "Top 25 Most Extraordinary Atlantans." South Fulton Lifestyle was named "Publication of the Year" in Atlanta two years in a row. Michelle has also been recognized for her work with youth in the community, and she received a Resolution from Rep. Roger Bruce and a Proclamation as "Outstanding Georgia Citizen" from Secretary of State Brad Ratffensperger.

Michelle created SoFu®, the name used to refer to the eight cities of South Fulton County. She also created the Moms All In® conference for female executives and entrepreneurs. She recently released the ebook version of this book, which has already reached 100s of families and started conversations about parenting.

CPSIA information can be obtained
at www.ICGtesting.com
Printed in the USA
LVHW091915100321
681105LV00025B/689/J